THE BRIDE OF CHRIST

A Contemplative Experience

THE BRIDE OF CHRIST

A Contemplative Experience

A Scripture-Rooted, Journey into
the Heart of Divine Love

Symbol & Silence
symbolandsilence.com

ISBN: 978-1-972088-01-2

"I am my beloved's and my beloved is mine."

Song of Solomon 6:3

Table of Contents

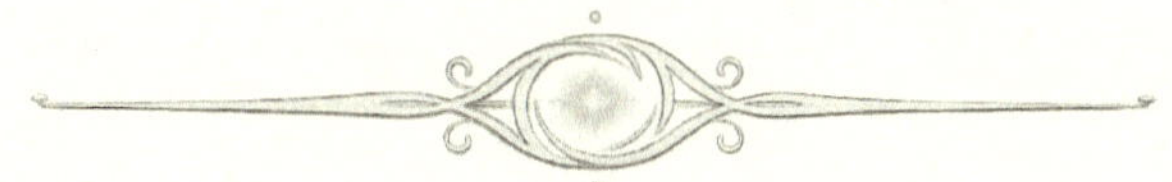

Welcome to the Journey

This *Symbol and Silence* Series, *The Bride of Christ*, invites you into a deeper exploration of the Christian life, not merely as belief or behavior, but as a love story unfolding between God and the human soul. In this study, *The Bride of Christ*, we turn our attention to one of Scripture's most intimate and transformative metaphors: God as the Divine Bridegroom, and the Church as His beloved.

In this study, the Bride of Christ is not treated as abstraction or metaphor, but as <u>the deepest truth</u> about who we are in relation to God. The imagery of covenant, desire, fidelity, and union becomes a mirror for the soul, illuminating the ways God draws us – sometimes gently, sometimes through desert seasons, always toward communion.

Each part of the series explores a movement of that journey:

- becoming aware of God's desire for us,
- learning the disciplines that cultivate intimacy,
- confronting the barriers to love,
- allowing the soul to be purified,
- entering into communion,
- and embracing the life of union to which Christ calls His Bride.

Entering the Experience

This guide is not designed to be rushed.

It is an invitation to slow down — to encounter Scripture not only with the mind, but with the whole person: body, attention, memory, and desire. Throughout the Christian contemplative tradition, believers have gathered in quiet spaces to listen for the voice of Christ with unhurried hearts. This study follows in that stream.

This particular guide is written for the leader who will gently guide a small group through the experience. While individuals may engage these practices on their own, the rhythm of this study is especially suited for communal use. The language, pacing, and moments of shared silence are designed to help a group settle together and listen together in God's presence.

For group settings, the ideal group size is between 4 and 10 participants. Smaller groups often allow for deeper quiet and more spacious sharing, while larger groups may require additional care to preserve the unhurried atmosphere. When possible, choose a group size that allows every voice to remain brief and every moment of silence to feel comfortable rather than crowded.

Many of us have learned to approach Scripture primarily through analysis, discussion, and information. These are valuable gifts. Yet there is another way of attending to God's Word – one that emphasizes presence before explanation, listening before response, and communion before conclusion.

In this experience, we practice that quieter way.

Each gathering follows a simple and repeatable rhythm. We settle the room. We allow the body to grow still. We listen to Scripture slowly and together. We notice what gently rises within us. And we rest in the promise that Christ is already present among His people.

Nothing here depends on special knowledge or spiritual expertise. Participants do not need to force insight, produce emotion, or achieve a particular state of mind. We come as we are, trusting that God often works most deeply in spaces that are calm, attentive, and unhurried.

Over the coming weeks, we will move through the central movements of the Bride of Christ: belonging, preparation, devotion, hope, and union.

These themes are not presented merely as ideas to understand, but as realities to inhabit together.

This way of gathering may feel unfamiliar at first. Silence may seem longer than expected. The pace may feel slower than what we are used to. If so, that is simply part of the settling. With each week, the rhythm becomes more natural, and the space more deeply received. Each reflection is designed to take 45 minutes.

We enter this journey with confidence in the One who calls us His own.

Christ is not distant. He is not hurried. He stands among His people – steady, attentive, and faithful.

We come to listen. We come to remain. We come as those who already belong.

How to Use These Materials

The Bride of Christ series is designed to accompany you on a spiritual journey – not only through Scripture, but through the landscape of your own soul. This guide is part of a larger ecosystem of formation resources offered through **Symbol & Silence**, each crafted to help pastors, small groups, and individual believers explore the mystery of union with God.

This book contains the complete set of contemplative experiences for the series. Symbol and Silence also offers bible studies and ministry guides for this series. Each week invites you into a different dimension of spiritual preparation – identity, desire, holiness, hope, communion, and union.

A Note on Timing

Each weekly gathering is designed to unfold over approximately **45 minutes**, following the natural rhythm of the contemplative experience. Groups are encouraged to allow an additional 10–15 minutes beforehand for informal arrival, greeting, and settling into the space.

The goal of this guide is not to move quickly, but to move attentively. If your group occasionally needs a few extra minutes to rest in silence or to share briefly, that is perfectly appropriate. The times below are offered simply as a gentle framework to help leaders pace the experience.

Suggested Weekly Flow

- Opening Gathering & Conversation — 10–12 minutes
- Settling Prayer & Silence — 3–5 minutes
- Guided Breathing — 5 minutes
- Lectio Divina Scripture Reading — 10 minutes
- Interior Noticing & Brief Sharing — 10 minutes
- Closing Prayer — 2–3 minutes

Leaders should feel free to hold the structure lightly. Some weeks may feel naturally quieter; others may invite slightly more shared reflection. The aim is not precision, but attentiveness to the movement of the group and the quiet work of the Spirit.

If the group is new to silence, the first week may feel slower or slightly unfamiliar. With time, most groups find that the rhythm becomes more natural and deeply welcomed.

Above all, resist the urge to rush.
The fruit of this practice often grows in the unhurried spaces.

The Bride of Christ Series

The Bride of Christ is part of a broader formation journey developed through Symbol & Silence. Each resource in this series is designed to follow the same theological vision and contemplative rhythm, allowing individuals, small groups, and churches to engage the material in ways that best support their context.

At the heart of every resource is the same conviction: the Christian life is not merely information to master, but a relationship to inhabit — a gradual preparation of the people of God for union with Christ.

To support that shared vision, Symbol & Silence offers several companion resources that mirror and extend the experience you encounter in this guide.

Ministry Leader Guide
The **Ministry Guide** equips pastors, teachers, and ministry leaders to confidently lead others through *The Bride of Christ* journey. It includes expanded teaching notes, theological framing, facilitation guidance, and

sermon preparation support. This resource is especially helpful for churches seeking to integrate the themes of the series into preaching, teaching, or coordinated formation efforts.

Weekly Reflections on Substack

The **Symbol & Silence Substack** offers ongoing narrative reflections that correspond to the movements of the series. These essays are freely available and are designed to prepare the heart, deepen theological imagination, and extend the contemplative posture into daily reading life. Many groups find these reflections helpful as a gentle entry point into each week's theme.

Contemporary Bible Study Edition

For groups that prefer a more discussion-forward format, the **Contemporary Bible Study** edition presents the same theological journey in a structure designed for conversational engagement. While the contemplative guide emphasizes silence and interior noticing, this version provides additional prompts and teaching movement suited to traditional small group settings.

Youth Group Curriculum

Recognizing the importance of forming younger believers, Symbol & Silence also offers a **Youth Group Curriculum** built on the same core themes of belonging, preparation, devotion, hope, and union. The youth materials translate the vision of *The Bride of Christ* into age-appropriate language and interactive experiences for middle school and high school settings.

Together, these resources allow churches and individuals to engage the same spiritual journey across multiple contexts and learning styles. Whether used individually or as a coordinated pathway, the aim remains the same – to help the people of God grow in attentive love, steady hope, and joyful readiness for the life we are being prepared to share with Christ.

A Word of Encouragement

Symbol and Silence rests on the conviction that Scripture is not merely a record of divine speech – it is an invitation into relationship. When read contemplatively, the text becomes the meeting place between the Divine Bridegroom and the human soul. We cross the boundary between doctrine and mystery, and the biblical narrative reveals itself not only as history, but as a love story in which we ourselves are the beloved.

As you begin, remember: this journey is not about mastery but intimacy. You are not being tested; you are being invited—to rest, to listen, to be known. Faith grows not by striving, but by remaining in the love that already holds you.

Welcome to the path.

May your soul find restoration in every step.

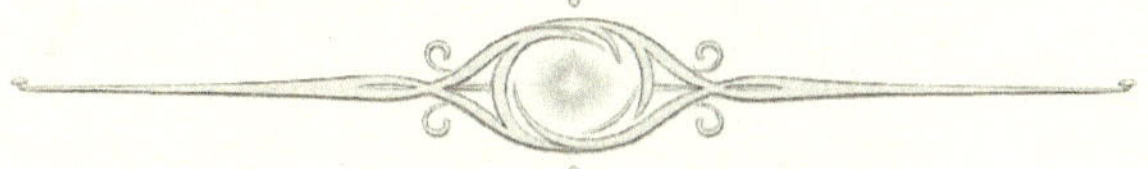

Preparation

Before we gather, we prepare a place of peace. We do this not to create God's presence, but to make room to notice it.

Throughout the Christian contemplative tradition, believers have set apart simple spaces where the body can settle and the heart can become attentive. A quiet environment helps us release urgency, soften distraction, and remember why we have come.

In this study, the space itself becomes an act of hospitality – a gentle signal that we are entering something unhurried, relational, and sacred.

Aim for an atmosphere that feels warm and welcoming, similar to a comfortable living room, while keeping the space visually simple and free from distraction.

Nothing elaborate is needed.

Simplicity is the goal.
Warmth is the aim.
Peace is the atmosphere we seek to offer one another.

Prepare the room with care.

Space Preparation Checklist

1. Lighting
    a. Soften overhead lighting if possible.
    b. Use warm lamps or natural light when available.
    c. Avoid harsh or bright illumination.
2. Temperature
    a. Set the room to a comfortable, moderate temperature.
    b. Avoid spaces that feel overly warm or noticeably cool.
    c. Adjust in advance so participants can settle without distraction.
3. Seating
    a. Arrange chairs in a simple circle.
    b. Remove tables or barriers between participants when possible.
    c. Ensure everyone sits at equal level.
    d. Choose seating that feels comfortable for extended sitting.
4. Atmosphere

   a. Create a space that feels calm and welcoming, similar to a quiet living room.
   b. Keep the room visually simple and uncluttered.
   c. Remove or cover distractions such as televisions, busy wall art, or unnecessary screens.
5. Focal Point
   a. Place a simple focal element at the center of the circle. (A candle, cross, open Bible, or chalice works well.)
   b. Keep the arrangement uncluttered and reverent.
   c. If using a candle, light it shortly before the gathering begins.
6. Sound
   a. Maintain a quiet room environment.
   b. If music is used before the gathering, keep it instrumental and low.
   c. Turn off music before the formal beginning.
7. Technology
   a. Silence your own phone.
   b. Invite participants to silence and set aside their devices upon arrival.
8. Leader Posture
   a. Arrive a few minutes early.
   b. Move calmly and without hurry.
   c. Greet participants warmly as they enter.
   d. Allow natural conversation during the arrival window.

When the space is prepared, trust its simplicity.

We are not trying to manufacture a moment. We are simply creating room to become attentive to the One who is already present among His people.

1

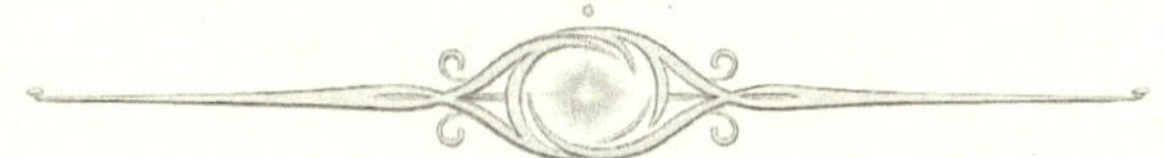

Mystical Union: The Ultimate Hope

Gathering Together

Read aloud.

We have come as we are.

The day has followed us into this room (the conversations, the responsibilities, the unfinished thoughts).

We do not need to push any of it away.

We simply arrive together.

Before we enter the quiet, we take a few moments to speak with one another. This brief conversation is not a time to analyze or solve, but simply to notice what is already present within us.

We listen with patience.
We speak with simplicity.
We leave generous space between voices.

Whole-Group Conversation

Read aloud.

Before the Bible ever speaks of Christian morality, spiritual gifts, church structure, or mission, it speaks of desire – God's desire to dwell with His people, and humanity's deep, often unspoken desire to dwell with God. From Genesis to Revelation, Scripture tells a single love story: the Creator forming, pursuing, restoring, and ultimately uniting Himself with His creation.

This concept is the foundation of Christian hope. It is what every promise of Scripture points toward. Paul calls it *"the mystery hidden for ages, now revealed… Christ in you, the hope of glory"* (Col. 1:26–27). Jesus describes it as abiding – "*I in you, and you in Me"* (John 15:4). Revelation ends with a wedding: *"The Spirit and the Bride say, Come"* (Rev. 22:17).

Every spiritual practice, every act of obedience, every moment of repentance or worship is ultimately ordered toward this one end: union with the One who loves us.

We begin here because this is where Scripture begins – not with rules to follow, but with a relationship to enter. Many Christians spend years trying to improve their spiritual lives without ever naming the longing beneath the surface: I want God. I want to be with Him and in Him, and I want Him to be in me.

This week's theme, Mystical Union, is meant to feel familiar, like something your soul has always known but perhaps never articulated. The early Christian teachers said that God places in every heart a homing instinct, a yearning for the One who made us. Union is not something we achieve; it is something we awaken to, yield to, and participate in.

As you begin, you are not learning a theory. You are stepping into the deepest truth about yourself: you were made for God, and God desires to make His home in you.

Let this week open the door.

Group Reflection

Read aloud.

In a moment, I will read a few discussion prompts. Each person will have a moment to share anything they would like to reflect. We will go around the room to provide each person with space, but nobody should feel like there is any pressure. If you have nothing to say, simply pass. As we share together:

- We keep our responses brief.
- We do not try to fix or correct one another.
- We allow moments of silence between speakers.
- We trust that simple honesty is enough.

Leader gently guides the group using the prompts below.

1. **Prompt 1**

   When we hear the image of being *the Bride of Christ*, what feelings or reactions naturally rise in us?

   Allow brief, unhurried sharing.

2. **Prompt 2**

   Where in our lives right now do we most long to know that we belong to God?

   Allow sharing. Do not rush to fill silence.

3. **Optional Prompt 3**

What sometimes makes it difficult to rest in God's love?

Use only if the conversation feels natural and unforced.

Transition to Stillness

Read aloud.

As our voices settle, we begin to turn our attention more fully toward God's presence among us.

Let us become still together.

Settling into Stillness

Read aloud.

As our voices quiet, we allow the room to grow still.

There is nothing we need to accomplish in this moment.
Nothing we need to prove.
Nothing we need to force.

We simply become present together.

Let us become still.

Pause here for 60–90 seconds of shared silence.

Allow the silence to feel unhurried. If the room feels slightly restless at first, do not rush forward. The settling is part of the work.

Opening Prayer

Read aloud.

Bridegroom of Your people,
You have drawn us here in love.

Quiet what is hurried within us.
Steady what feels unsettled.

As we breathe and listen together,
help us to rest in Your presence —
not striving,
not performing,
simply received in Your care.

We gather as those who belong to You.

Amen.

Becoming Aware of the Breath

Read aloud.

We remain seated in stillness.

Feet grounded.
Hands resting gently.

If it feels comfortable, we allow our eyes to close.

We begin by simply noticing the breath.

Air entering.
Air leaving.

After a few natural breaths, we allow the rhythm to slow slightly.

We inhale gently through the nose.
We exhale slowly through the nose.

If it feels natural, let the exhale be just a little longer than the inhale.

There is no need to force the breath.
We are not trying to breathe perfectly.

We are simply allowing the body to settle into a quieter rhythm.

Inhale… slowly.

Exhale… gently.

Unhurried.

Steady.

Present.

Remain here for about 2–3 minutes.

If the mind begins to wander, simply return our attention to the quiet rhythm of the breath.

In this gentle awareness, we allow the body to soften . . . and the heart to become attentive.

Breathing the Prayer

Read aloud.

Continue breathing slowly and gently.

Keeping the same quiet rhythm we have already found, begin to let a simple prayer accompany the rhythm.

As we inhale slowly through the nose, we pray silently:

You are here.

As we exhale gently:

We are Yours.

Inhale…

You are here.

Exhale…

We are Yours.

We do not rush the words.

If the breath and the words do not match perfectly, we let the words soften and follow the natural rhythm of the breath.

We remain unhurried.

Continue for several breaths.

The Breath of Belonging

Now we allow the deeper promise to rest on the breath.

As we inhale:

We are our Beloved's…

As we exhale:

…and our Beloved is ours.

Slowly.

Gently.

Steady and unforced.

Again.

Inhale…

We are our Beloved's…

Exhale…

…and our Beloved is ours.

If the mind wanders, we simply return.

If the words fade for a moment, we begin again.

We are not trying to create closeness.

We are resting in what has already been spoken over us.

Remain here for several breaths.

The Breath of Quiet

Now, release the words.

We continue breathing slowly and gently.

Christ stands among His people – steady, attentive, near.

We rest together in the quiet.

Remain in silence for about 60–90 seconds.

Re-Gathering

Together, softly, we say once:

We are our Beloved's, and our Beloved is ours.

We let the words settle.

And we remain still.

Hearing the Word

Read aloud.

We remain seated in stillness.

Our breathing stays slow and gentle.

We do not hurry this moment.

As the Scripture is read, we listen together.

We are not listening to analyze. We are not listening to master the text.

We are simply receiving the words as they are spoken among us.

If a word or phrase draws our attention, we notice it gently and let it remain.

Stay relaxed.
Stay unhurried.
Stay present.

Scripture Readings

- **Ephesians 5: 25-27**
  Leader reads slowly and clearly.

Husbands, love your wives, just as Christ loved the church and gave himself up for her to make her holy, cleansing her by the washing with water through the word, and to present her to himself as a radiant church, without stain or wrinkle or any other blemish, but holy and blameless.

(Pause in silence — about 20–30 seconds.)

(Read again, slightly more slowly.)

(Longer silence — about 30–45 seconds.)

(Read a third time, unhurried and steady.)

(Remain in silence — about 60 seconds.)

(Repeat the same exercise with any of these additional scriptures)

- **John 17: 20-23**
  "My prayer is not for them alone. I pray also for those who will believe in me through their message, that all of them may be one, Father, just as you are in me and I am in you. May they also be in us so that the world may believe that you have sent me. I have given them the glory that you gave me, that they may be one as we are one – I in them and you in me – so that they may be

brought to complete unity. Then the world will know that you sent me and have loved them even as you have loved me.

- **2 Peter 1: 3-4**

  His divine power has given us everything we need for a godly life through our knowledge of him who called us by his own glory and goodness. Through these he has given us his very great and precious promises, so that through them you may participate in the divine nature, having escaped the corruption in the world caused by evil desires.

Interior Noticing

Read aloud.

We remain in the quiet for a moment longer.

There is nothing we need to figure out.

We simply notice what has gently risen within us as we listened.

We stay relaxed.
We stay unhurried.
We remain attentive.

Gentle Reflection

Without forcing words, notice:

What word or phrase quietly drew our attention?

(Pause. Allow silence first before any sharing.)

If it feels natural, we may briefly speak the word or phrase that stood out to us.

We keep our sharing simple and unhurried.

After a few responses or a short pause, continue.

Where did we sense warmth . . . or perhaps a place of resistance?

Pause again. Allow brief sharing if appropriate.

We do not need to explain why.

We simply notice.

After another pause.

What, if anything, felt like invitation?

Allow silence to carry this moment.

Holding the Moment

We resist the urge to analyze or resolve.

God often speaks most clearly in what quietly lingers.

We allow what has surfaced to remain gently before Him.

Short silence — about 30–45 seconds.

Receiving the Promise

Together, softly, we say:

We are our Beloved's, and our Beloved is ours.

Repeat once more, slowly.

We are our Beloved's, and our Beloved is ours.

We let the words settle among us.

Brief silence.

Closing Prayer

Read aloud

Faithful Bridegroom,

You have drawn us near in love. Before we could reach for You, You had already set Your heart upon us.

Keep us steady in this promise.
Quiet what remains anxious within us.
Strengthen what is still learning to trust.

As we leave this space,
teach us to remember what is already true:

We are our Beloved's,
and our Beloved is ours.

Amen.

Resting in the Quiet

We remain together in stillness for one final moment.

When the time feels right, the leader may softly say:

We return gently to one another.

Participants may slowly open their eyes.

Take a moment to notice the room again.

Notice one another.

When ready, simple conversation may resume naturally.

There is no need to rush away.

2

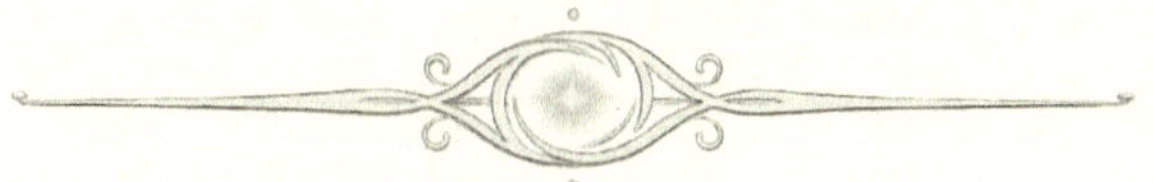

Getting Ready for the Big Day

Gathering Together

Read aloud

We have come as we are.

The day has followed us into this room (the conversations, the responsibilities, the unfinished thoughts).

We do not need to push any of it away.

We simply arrive together.

Before we enter the quiet, we take a few moments to speak with one another. This brief conversation is not a time to analyze or solve, but simply to notice what is already present within us.

We listen with patience.
We speak with simplicity.
We leave generous space between voices.

Whole-Group Conversation

Read aloud

All great relationships move toward commitment, and commitment requires readiness. Scripture describes the Church, the collective people of God, as a bride being prepared for her wedding day. This is the Bible's most comprehensive picture of salvation.

In the ancient world, a bride did not prepare for her wedding by purchasing decorations or planning a ceremony. Her preparation was transformational: she learned how to live in harmony with the one she would marry. She cultivated beauty of character, steadiness of soul, and a heart oriented toward love and mutual belonging. The wedding was not merely an event; it was the culmination of a process.

Likewise, the Christian life is a betrothal season, in which the soul gradually lets go of what cannot coexist with love, and grows in what can.

Paul says that Christ is forming His people *"without spot or wrinkle… holy and without blemish"* (Eph. 5:27). This is not pressure but promise. The transformation is God's work in us, yet it unfolds in cooperation with our desire.

Preparation is not about perfectionism or religious performance; it is about clearing space. It is about choosing to orient heart, mind, habits, and imagination toward the One who loves us.

This stage can be described as "ordering the affections." Like a bride laying aside distractions so she can attend to the voice of her beloved, the soul begins to sift its priorities. What leads me toward God? What draws me away? What creates space for intimacy? What clutters it?

Preparation is an act of love. It is the joyful anticipation of what is coming. It is the soul saying, "I want to be ready when You arrive."

In this reflection, we explore the preparation that is taking place in each of us. The Christian journey not as mastering spiritual tasks, but as adorning the soul for the One it loves. This week is about discovering that readiness is less about effort and more about desire – less about proving ourselves, and more about opening ourselves.

Let this week awaken expectant love.

Group Reflection

Read aloud

In a moment, I will read a few discussion prompts. Each person will have a moment to share anything they would like to reflect. We will go around the room to provide each person with space, but nobody should feel like there is any pressure. If you have nothing to say, simply pass. As we share together:

- We keep our responses brief.
- We do not try to fix or correct one another.
- We allow moments of silence between speakers.
- We trust that simple honesty is enough.

Leader gently guides the group using the prompts below.

1. **Prompt 1**
   When you hear the image of *preparing for a wedding day*, what feelings or impressions naturally rise in you?

   Allow brief, unhurried sharing.

2. **Prompt 2**
   Where in your life right now do you sense God may be quietly inviting you to make more space for Him?

   Allow sharing. Do not rush to fill silence.

3. **Optional Prompt 3**

   What distractions or patterns most often pull your attention away from the deeper life of love with God?

   Use only if the conversation feels natural and unforced.

Transition to Stillness

Read aloud

As our voices settle, we begin to turn our attention more fully toward God's presence among us.

Let us become still together.

Settling into Stillness

Read aloud

As our voices quiet, we allow the room to grow still.

There is nothing we need to accomplish in this moment.
Nothing we need to prove.
Nothing we need to force.

We simply become present together.

Let us become still.

Pause here for 60–90 seconds of shared silence.

Allow the silence to feel unhurried. If the room feels slightly restless at first, do not rush forward. The settling is part of the work.

Opening Prayer

Read aloud

Faithful Bridegroom,

You have called us into Your love.
As we gather again in Your presence, quiet what feels hurried within us and steady what feels divided.

Where our hearts are crowded, make room.

Where our attention is scattered, draw it gently back toward You.

Form in us a deeper readiness, not through pressure,
but through desire awakened by Your Spirit.

Teach us to welcome the quiet work you are already doing within us.

We belong to You, and we trust the love that prepares us.

Amen.

Becoming Aware of the Breath

Read aloud

We remain seated in stillness.

Feet grounded.
Hands resting gently.

If it feels comfortable, we allow our eyes to close.

We begin by simply noticing the breath.

Air entering.
Air leaving.

After a few natural breaths, we allow the rhythm to slow slightly.

We inhale gently through the nose.
We exhale slowly through the nose.

If it feels natural, let the exhale be just a little longer than the inhale.

There is no need to force the breath.
We are not trying to breathe perfectly.

We are simply allowing the body to settle into a quieter rhythm.

Inhale… slowly.
Exhale… gently.

Unhurried.
Steady.
Present.

Remain here for about 2–3 minutes.

If the mind begins to wander, simply return our attention to the quiet rhythm of the breath.

In this gentle awareness, we allow the body to soften . . . and the heart to become attentive.

Breathing the Prayer

Read aloud

Continue breathing slowly and gently.

Keeping the same quiet rhythm we have already found, begin to let a simple prayer accompany the rhythm.

As we inhale slowly through the nose, we pray silently:

You are here.

As we exhale gently:

We are Yours.

Inhale…

You are here.

Exhale…

We are Yours.

We do not rush the words.

If the breath and the words do not match perfectly, we let the words soften and follow the natural rhythm of the breath.

We remain unhurried.

Continue for several breaths.

The Breath of Belonging

Now we allow the deeper promise to rest on the breath.

As we inhale:

We are our Beloved's…

As we exhale:

…and our Beloved is ours.

Slowly.

Gently.

Steady and unforced.

Again.

Inhale…

We are our Beloved's…

Exhale…

…and our Beloved is ours.

If the mind wanders, we simply return.

If the words fade for a moment, we begin again.

We are not trying to create closeness.

We are resting in what has already been spoken over us.

Remain here for several breaths.

The Breath of Quiet

Now, release the words.

We continue breathing slowly and gently.

Christ stands among His people – steady, attentive, near.

We rest together in the quiet.

Remain in silence for about 60–90 seconds.

Re-Gathering

Together, softly, we say once:

We are our Beloved's, and our Beloved is ours.

We let the words settle.

And we remain still.

Hearing the Word

Read aloud

We remain seated in stillness.

Our breathing stays slow and gentle.

We do not hurry this moment.

As the Scripture is read, we listen together.

We are not listening to analyze. We are not listening to master the text.

We are simply receiving the words as they are spoken among us.

If a word or phrase draws our attention, we notice it gently and let it remain.

Stay relaxed.
Stay unhurried.
Stay present.

Scripture Readings

- **Romans 12: 1 – 2**

Leader reads slowly and clearly.

Therefore, I urge you, brothers and sisters, in view of God's mercy, to offer your bodies as a living sacrifice, holy and pleasing to God – this is your true and proper worship. Do not conform to the pattern of this world, but be transformed by the renewing of your mind. Then you will be able to test and approve what God's will is—his good, pleasing and perfect will.

Pause in silence — about 20–30 seconds.

Leader reads again, slightly more slowly.

Longer silence — about 30–45 seconds.

Leader reads a third time, unhurried and steady.

Remain in silence — about 60 seconds.

Repeat the same exercise with any of these additional scriptures

- **2 Corinthians 3:18**
  And we all, who with unveiled faces contemplate the Lord's glory, are being transformed into his image with ever-increasing glory, which comes from the Lord, who is the Spirit.

- **Philippians 1: 3 – 6**
  In all my prayers for all of you, I always pray with joy because of your partnership in the gospel from the first day until now, being confident of this, that he who began a good work in you will carry it on to completion until the day of Christ Jesus.

Interior Noticing

Read aloud

We remain in the quiet for a moment longer.

There is nothing we need to figure out.

We simply notice what has gently risen within us as we listened.

We stay relaxed.
We stay unhurried.
We remain attentive.

Gentle Reflection

Without forcing words, notice:

What word or phrase quietly drew our attention?

Pause. Allow silence first before any sharing.

If it feels natural, we may briefly speak the word or phrase that stood out to us.

We keep our sharing simple and unhurried.

After a few responses or a short pause, continue.

Where did we sense warmth . . . or perhaps a place of resistance?

Pause again. Allow brief sharing if appropriate.

We do not need to explain why.

We simply notice.

After another pause.

What, if anything, felt like invitation?

Allow silence to carry this moment.

Holding the Moment

We resist the urge to analyze or resolve.

God often speaks most clearly in what quietly lingers.

We allow what has surfaced to remain gently before Him.

Short silence — about 30–45 seconds.

Receiving the Promise

Together, softly, we say:

We are our Beloved's, and our Beloved is ours.

Repeat once more, slowly.

We are our Beloved's, and our Beloved is ours.

We let the words settle among us.

Brief silence.

Closing Prayer

Read aloud

Faithful Bridegroom,

You are gently preparing Your people in love.
Where we have tried to hurry the work, teach us to trust Your pace.

Where we have felt unready or unsure, steady us in the promise that You are faithful to complete what You have begun.

Order our affections. Quiet what competes for our attention. Draw our hearts more fully toward You.

Make us a people who are watchful in hope and open in love.

We rest in Your care, trusting the quiet work of Your Spirit within us.

Amen.

Resting in the Quiet

We remain together in stillness for one final moment.

When the time feels right, the leader may softly say:

We return gently to one another.

Participants may slowly open their eyes.

Take a moment to notice the room again.

Notice one another.

When ready, simple conversation may resume naturally.

There is no need to rush away.

3

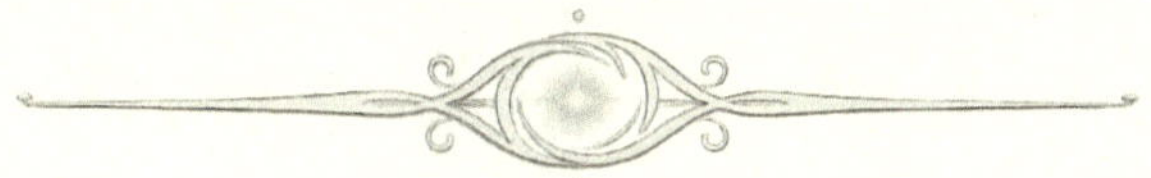

Forsaking All Others

Gathering Together

Read aloud

We have come as we are.

The day has followed us into this room (the conversations, the responsibilities, the unfinished thoughts).

We do not need to push any of it away.

We simply arrive together.
Before we enter the quiet, we take a few moments to speak with one another. This brief conversation is not a time to analyze or solve, but simply to notice what is already present within us.

We listen with patience.
We speak with simplicity.
We leave generous space between voices.

Whole-Group Conversation

Read aloud

In the previous week, we reflected on the Christian life as a season of preparation. This week brings us closer to the heart of that preparation: the quiet call to *forsake all others.*

At first hearing, the phrase can sound severe. Yet in the language of Scripture – and in the life of the soul – it is not primarily an act of loss. It is an act of devotion. It is the gentle clearing of the inner room so that love may dwell there without division.

In the ancient world, betrothal involved a decisive turning of the heart. A bride's life began to reflect where her deepest loyalty rested. Her waiting was not empty time; it was a season of becoming – of learning to live with her affection steadily oriented toward the one she loved.

Scripture gives this image to the Church. We are a people being drawn into a more undivided love for God.

To *forsake all others* does not mean withdrawing from relationships, responsibilities, or the ordinary joys of life. Rather, it means gently refusing to let anything else occupy the place that belongs to God alone. It is the quiet reordering of the heart's center of gravity.

This movement often brings new clarity. As love for God deepens, we begin noticing attachments that once felt invisible – our need for approval, desire to control outcomes, subtle ways we anchor our identity in success, security, or self-protection. Like shadows becoming visible in increasing light, these patterns come into view, inviting us into freedom.

This is the beginning of purification. The soul is being made more spacious, more whole, more capable of communion. Forsaking all others is not subtraction. It is alignment. It is the quiet learning of the heart to say, with growing trust:

My life belongs to the One who first loved me.

As you enter this week, hold this steady reassurance: God does not remove what is good in order to diminish us. He gently loosens only what keeps us from receiving more of His life.

May this week bring clarity to your desires, simplicity to your loves, and a deeper rest in the One to whom you already belong.

Group Reflection

Read aloud

In a moment, I will read a few discussion prompts. Each person will have a moment to share anything they would like to reflect. We will go around the room to provide each person with space, but nobody should feel like there is any pressure. If you have nothing to say, simply pass. As we share together:

- We keep our responses brief.
- We do not try to fix or correct one another.
- We allow moments of silence between speakers.
- We trust that simple honesty is enough.

Leader gently guides the group using the prompts below.

1. **Prompt 1**
   When you hear the phrase *"forsaking all others,"* what feelings or images first rise within you?

   (Allow brief, unhurried sharing.)

2. **Prompt 2**
   Where in your life do you most sense the tension between divided attention and wholehearted love for God?

   (Allow sharing. Do not rush to fill silence.)

3. **Optional Prompt 3**

   What would it feel like for your love for God to become more simple and undivided in this season?

   (Use only if the conversation feels natural and unforced.)

Transition to Stillness

Leader says the following

As our voices settle, we begin to turn our attention more fully toward God's presence among us.

Let us become still together.

Settling into Stillness

Read aloud

As our voices quiet, we allow the room to grow still.

There is nothing we need to accomplish in this moment.
Nothing we need to prove.
Nothing we need to force.

We simply become present together.

Let us become still.

Pause here for 60–90 seconds of shared silence.

Allow the silence to feel unhurried. If the room feels slightly restless at first, do not rush forward. The settling is part of the work.

Opening Prayer

Read aloud

Faithful Bridegroom,

You who love us with a steady and undivided love, draw near to us again. As we gather in Your presence, quiet what feels crowded within us and gently bring into the light whatever keeps our hearts divided.

Where we have held tightly to lesser things, loosen our grip with Your kindness. Where our loves have become scattered, draw them back toward their true center in You.

We do not come to strive or to prove ourselves. We come to be made more whole by the mercy of Your presence.

Give us courage to notice, grace to release, and trust to rest in the love that is already holding us. We belong to You, and we welcome the quiet work of Your Spirit.

Amen.

Becoming Aware of the Breath

Leader reads the breath work instructions.

We remain seated in stillness.

Feet grounded.
Hands resting gently.

If it feels comfortable, we allow our eyes to close.

We begin by simply noticing the breath.

Air entering.
Air leaving.

After a few natural breaths, we allow the rhythm to slow slightly.

We inhale gently through the nose.
We exhale slowly through the nose.

If it feels natural, let the exhale be just a little longer than the inhale.

There is no need to force the breath.
We are not trying to breathe perfectly.

We are simply allowing the body to settle into a quieter rhythm.

Inhale… slowly.
Exhale… gently.

Unhurried.
Steady.
Present.

(Remain here for about 2–3 minutes.)

If the mind begins to wander, simply return our attention to the quiet rhythm of the breath.

In this gentle awareness, we allow the body to soften . . . and the heart to become attentive.

Breathing the Prayer

Read aloud

Continue breathing slowly and gently.

Keeping the same quiet rhythm we have already found, begin to let a simple prayer accompany the rhythm.

As we inhale slowly through the nose, we pray silently:

You are here.

As we exhale gently:

We are Yours.

Inhale…

You are here.

Exhale…

We are Yours.

We do not rush the words.

If the breath and the words do not match perfectly, we let the words soften and follow the natural rhythm of the breath.

We remain unhurried.

(Continue for several breaths.)

The Breath of Belonging

Now we allow the deeper promise to rest on the breath.

As we inhale:

We are our Beloved's…

As we exhale:

…and our Beloved is ours.

Slowly.

Gently.

Steady and unforced.

Again.

Inhale…

We are our Beloved's…

Exhale…

…and our Beloved is ours.

If the mind wanders, we simply return.

If the words fade for a moment, we begin again.

We are not trying to create closeness.

We are resting in what has already been spoken over us.

(Remain here for several breaths.)

The Breath of Quiet

Now, release the words.

We continue breathing slowly and gently.

Christ stands among His people – steady, attentive, near.

We rest together in the quiet.

(Remain in silence for about 60–90 seconds.)

Re-Gathering

Together, softly, we say once:

We are our Beloved's, and our Beloved is ours.

We let the words settle.

And we remain still.

Hearing the Word

Read aloud

We remain seated in stillness.

Our breathing stays slow and gentle.

We do not hurry this moment.

As the Scripture is read, we listen together.

We are not listening to analyze. We are not listening to master the text.

We are simply receiving the words as they are spoken among us.

If a word or phrase draws our attention, we notice it gently and let it remain.

Stay relaxed.
Stay unhurried.
Stay present.

Scripture Readings

- **Matthew 6: 19 - 21**

Leader reads slowly and clearly.

Do not store up for yourselves treasures on earth, where moths and vermin destroy, and where thieves break in and steal. But store up for yourselves treasures in heaven, where moths and vermin do not destroy, and where thieves do not break in and steal. For where your treasure is, there your heart will be also.

Pause in silence — about 20–30 seconds.

Leader reads again, slightly more slowly.

Longer silence — about 30–45 seconds.

Leader reads a third time, unhurried and steady.

Remain in silence — about 60 seconds.

Repeat the same exercise with any of these additional scriptures

- **Hebrews 12: 1 – 3**

Therefore, since we are surrounded by such a great cloud of witnesses, let us throw off everything that hinders and the sin that so easily entangles. And let us run with perseverance the race marked out for us, [2] fixing our eyes on Jesus, the pioneer and perfecter of faith. For the joy set before him he endured the cross, scorning its shame, and sat down at the right hand of the throne of God. [3] Consider him who endured such opposition from sinners, so that you will not grow weary and lose heart.

- **Psalm 73: 25 – 26**

  Whom have I in heaven but you?
  And earth has nothing I desire besides you.
  My flesh and my heart may fail,
  but God is the strength of my heart
  and my portion forever.

Interior Noticing

Read aloud

We remain in the quiet for a moment longer.

There is nothing we need to figure out.

We simply notice what has gently risen within us as we listened.

We stay relaxed.
We stay unhurried.
We remain attentive.

Gentle Reflection

Without forcing words, notice:

What word or phrase quietly drew our attention?

(Pause. Allow silence first before any sharing.)

If it feels natural, we may briefly speak the word or phrase that stood out to us.

We keep our sharing simple and unhurried.

(After a few responses or a short pause, continue.)

Where did we sense warmth . . . or perhaps a place of resistance?

(Pause again. Allow brief sharing if appropriate.)

We do not need to explain why.

We simply notice.

(After another pause.)

What, if anything, felt like invitation?

(Allow silence to carry this moment.)

Holding the Moment

We resist the urge to analyze or resolve.

God often speaks most clearly in what quietly lingers.

We allow what has surfaced to remain gently before Him.

(Short silence — about 30–45 seconds.)

Receiving the Promise

Together, softly, we say:

We are our Beloved's, and our Beloved is ours.

(Repeat once more, slowly.)

We are our Beloved's, and our Beloved is ours.

We let the words settle among us.

(Brief silence.)

Closing Prayer

Read aloud

Faithful Bridegroom,

You see our hearts with perfect gentleness. Thank You for the quiet ways You are drawing us into a more undivided love.

Where we still feel pulled in many directions, bring Your steadying peace. Where old attachments cling closely, loosen them with Your kindness.

Give us grace to treasure what leads us toward You, and freedom to release what does not.

Form in us a simpler love – not strained or fearful, but spacious and at rest in You.

We belong to You, and we trust the patient work of Your Spirit within us.

Amen.

Resting in the Quiet

We remain together in stillness for one final moment.

(When the time feels right, the leader may softly say:)

We return gently to one another.

Participants may slowly open their eyes.

Take a moment to notice the room again.

Notice one another.

When ready, simple conversation may resume naturally.

There is no need to rush away.

4

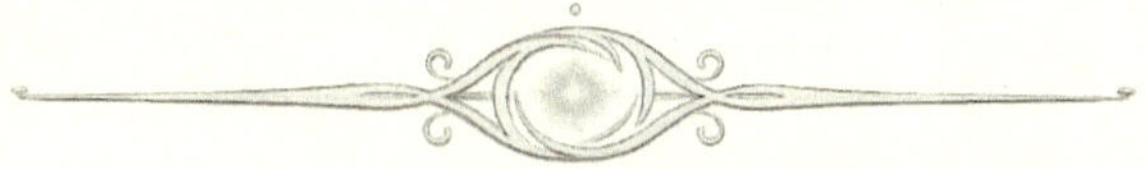

Hope in the Midst of a Broken World

Gathering Together

Read aloud

We have come as we are.

The day has followed us into this room (the conversations, the responsibilities, the unfinished thoughts).

We do not need to push any of it away.

We simply arrive together.

Before we enter the quiet, we take a few moments to speak with one another. This brief conversation is not a time to analyze or solve, but simply to notice what is already present within us.

We listen with patience.
We speak with simplicity.
We leave generous space between voices.

Whole-Group Conversation

Read aloud

By this point in the journey, we have begun to see the Christian life more clearly. We have heard the invitation to belong. We have felt the quiet work of preparation. We have begun the gentle work of simplifying our loves.

And yet, the world around us remains what it is.

Scripture never asks us to pretend that life is untouched by sorrow, uncertainty, or loss. The path of love does not remove us from the realities of a wounded world. Instead, it forms within us a different kind of steadiness as we live faithfully within it.

This week, we turn our attention to hope.

Not the fragile hope that depends on circumstances turning in our favor. Not the restless hope that demands quick resolution. But the deeper hope that allows the soul to remain rooted in love even when the surrounding landscape feels uncertain or incomplete.

In the language of Scripture, this hope is often expressed through the word *abide*. To abide is to remain. To stay. To dwell with quiet trust in the presence of the One who holds all things together.

The Bride does not wait in panic. She waits in confidence in the character of the One who has pledged Himself to her. Her hope is not built on perfect conditions, but on faithful love.

In our own lives, this kind of hope often grows in the very places where we would least expect it—amid disappointment, unanswered questions, and seasons that feel unresolved. Here, the Spirit forms in us a steadiness that is not easily shaken.

This week is an invitation to notice where you are being called to abide more deeply. It is an invitation to release the need for immediate clarity and to rest instead in the quiet faithfulness of God.

As we enter this time together, we do not deny the brokenness of the world. We simply refuse to let it have the final word.

Love remains.

Christ remains.
And we remain in Him.

May this week strengthen your quiet hope, steady your waiting, and deepen your trust in the One who is faithful in every season.

Group Reflection

Read aloud

In a moment, I will read a few discussion prompts. Each person will have a moment to share anything they would like to reflect. We will go around the room to provide each person with space, but nobody should feel like there is any pressure. If you have nothing to say, simply pass. As we share together:

- We keep our responses brief.
- We do not try to fix or correct one another.
- We allow moments of silence between speakers.
- We trust that simple honesty is enough.

(Leader gently guides the group using the prompts below.)

1. **Prompt 1**

   When you hear the invitation to *abide* in the midst of a broken world, what response or emotion first rises within you?

   Allow brief, unhurried sharing.

2. **Prompt 2**

   Where in your life right now are you being invited to remain faithful even while things feel unresolved?

   Allow sharing. Do not rush to fill silence.

3. **Optional Prompt 3**

   What helps your heart stay steady in love when circumstances around you feel uncertain?

   Use only if the conversation feels natural and unforced.

Transition to Stillness

Read aloud

As our voices settle, we begin to turn our attention more fully toward God's presence among us.

Let us become still together.

Settling into Stillness

Read aloud

As our voices quiet, we allow the room to grow still.

There is nothing we need to accomplish in this moment.
Nothing we need to prove.
Nothing we need to force.

We simply become present together.

Let us become still.

Pause here for 60–90 seconds of shared silence.

Allow the silence to feel unhurried. If the room feels slightly restless at first, do not rush forward. The settling is part of the work.

Opening Prayer

Read aloud

Faithful Bridegroom,

You remain with us in every season. As we gather in Your presence, meet us in the places that still feel uncertain and steady what feels unsettled within us.

In a world that is often hurried and fractured, teach us the quiet strength of abiding.

Where we are tempted to grow weary, renew our hope. Where we long for quick answers, teach us to rest in Your faithful love.

Form in us a patience that is rooted in trust and a hope that does not depend on circumstances.

We belong to You, and we remain in the care of Your presence.

Amen.

Becoming Aware of the Breath

Read aloud

We remain seated in stillness.

Feet grounded.
Hands resting gently.

If it feels comfortable, we allow our eyes to close..

We begin by simply noticing the breath.

Air entering.
Air leaving.

After a few natural breaths, we allow the rhythm to slow slightly.

We inhale gently through the nose.
We exhale slowly through the nose.

If it feels natural, let the exhale be just a little longer than the inhale.

There is no need to force the breath.
We are not trying to breathe perfectly.

We are simply allowing the body to settle into a quieter rhythm.

Inhale… slowly.
Exhale… gently.

Unhurried.
Steady.
Present.

Remain here for about 2–3 minutes.

If the mind begins to wander, simply return our attention to the quiet rhythm of the breath.

In this gentle awareness, we allow the body to soften . . . and the heart to become attentive.

Breathing the Prayer

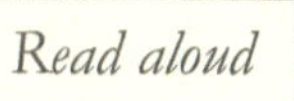

Continue breathing slowly and gently.

Keeping the same quiet rhythm we have already found, begin to let a simple prayer accompany the rhythm.

As we inhale slowly through the nose, we pray silently:

You are here.

As we exhale gently:

We are Yours.

Inhale…

You are here.

Exhale…

We are Yours.

We do not rush the words.

If the breath and the words do not match perfectly, we let the words soften and follow the natural rhythm of the breath.

We remain unhurried.

Continue for several breaths.

The Breath of Belonging

Now we allow the deeper promise to rest on the breath.

As we inhale:

We are our Beloved's…

As we exhale:

…and our Beloved is ours.

Slowly.

Gently.

Steady and unforced.

Again.

Inhale…

We are our Beloved's…

Exhale…

…and our Beloved is ours.

If the mind wanders, we simply return.

If the words fade for a moment, we begin again.

We are not trying to create closeness.

We are resting in what has already been spoken over us.

Remain here for several breaths.

The Breath of Quiet

Now, release the words.

We continue breathing slowly and gently.

Christ stands among His people – steady, attentive, near.

We rest together in the quiet.

Remain in silence for about 60–90 seconds.

Re-Gathering

Together, softly, we say once:

We are our Beloved's, and our Beloved is ours.

We let the words settle.

And we remain still.

Hearing the Word

Read aloud

We remain seated in stillness.

Our breathing stays slow and gentle.

We do not hurry this moment.

As the Scripture is read, we listen together.

We are not listening to analyze. We are not listening to master the text.

We are simply receiving the words as they are spoken among us.

If a word or phrase draws our attention, we notice it gently and let it remain.

Stay relaxed.
Stay unhurried.
Stay present.

Scripture Readings

- **John 15: 4 – 5**

  Leader reads slowly and clearly.

  Remain in me, as I also remain in you. No branch can bear fruit by itself; it must remain in the vine. Neither can you bear fruit unless you remain in me. I am the vine; you are the branches. If you remain in me and I in you, you will bear much fruit; apart from me you can do nothing.

Pause in silence — about 20–30 seconds.

Leader reads again, slightly more slowly.

Longer silence — about 30–45 seconds.

Leader reads a third time, unhurried and steady.

Remain in silence — about 60 seconds.

Repeat the same exercise with any of these additional scriptures:

- **Romans 8: 22 – 25**

  We know that the whole creation has been groaning as in the pains of childbirth right up to the present time. Not only so, but we ourselves, who have the firstfruits of the Spirit, groan inwardly as we wait eagerly for our adoption to sonship, the redemption of our bodies. For in this hope we were saved. But hope that is seen is no hope at all. Who hopes for what they already have? But if we hope for what we do not yet have, we wait for it patiently.

- **Lamentations 3: 22 – 24**

  Because of the Lord's great love we are not consumed,
  for his compassions never fail.

They are new every morning;
great is your faithfulness.
I say to myself, "The Lord is my portion;
therefore I will wait for him."

Interior Noticing

Read aloud

We remain in the quiet for a moment longer.

There is nothing we need to figure out.

We simply notice what has gently risen within us as we listened.

We stay relaxed.
We stay unhurried.
We remain attentive.

Gentle Reflection
Without forcing words, notice:

What word or phrase quietly drew our attention?

Pause. Allow silence first before any sharing.

If it feels natural, we may briefly speak the word or phrase that stood out to us.

We keep our sharing simple and unhurried.

After a few responses or a short pause, continue.

Where did we sense warmth . . . or perhaps a place of resistance?

Pause again. Allow brief sharing if appropriate.

We do not need to explain why.

We simply notice.

After another pause.

What, if anything, felt like invitation?

Allow silence to carry this moment.

Holding the Moment

We resist the urge to analyze or resolve.

God often speaks most clearly in what quietly lingers.

We allow what has surfaced to remain gently before Him.

Short silence — about 30–45 seconds.

Receiving the Promise

Together, softly, we say:

We are our Beloved's, and our Beloved is ours.

Repeat once more, slowly.

We are our Beloved's, and our Beloved is ours.

We let the words settle among us.

Brief silence.

Closing Prayer

Leader reads the closing prayer.

Faithful Bridegroom,

You remain with us in every season. In a world that often feels uncertain, thank You for the quiet steadiness of Your presence.

Where our hearts grow weary in the waiting, renew us with Your faithful love. Where we are tempted to rush ahead or withdraw in fear, teach us the grace of abiding.

Root our hope more deeply in You – not in changing circumstances, but in Your unchanging mercy.

Make us a people who remain, who trust, and who continue in love even when the path is not yet complete.

We belong to You, and we rest in the faithfulness that holds us.

Amen.

Resting in the Quiet

We remain together in stillness for one final moment.

When the time feels right, the leader may softly say:

We return gently to one another.

Participants may slowly open their eyes.

Take a moment to notice the room again.

Notice one another.

When ready, simple conversation may resume naturally.

There is no need to rush away.

5

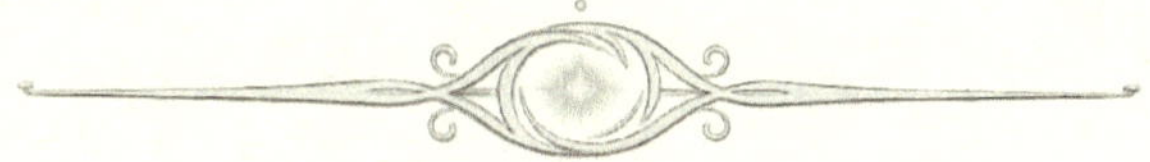

The Wedding Feast

Gathering Together

Read aloud

We have come as we are.

The day has followed us into this room (the conversations, the responsibilities, the unfinished thoughts).

We do not need to push any of it away.

We simply arrive together.

Before we enter the quiet, we take a few moments to speak with one another. This brief conversation is not a time to analyze or solve, but simply to notice what is already present within us.

We listen with patience.
We speak with simplicity.
We leave generous space between voices.

Whole-Group Conversation

Leader reads the context to the group.

Throughout Scripture, the kingdom of God is often described not merely as an idea to understand, but as a feast to enter – a table prepared, a gathering called, a celebration already set in motion. At the center of this great promise stands the Bridegroom, welcoming His Bride into the fullness of shared life.

This final movement turns our attention toward that union.

The image of the wedding feast reveals something essential about the heart of God. He is not preparing His people for mere survival, nor only for endurance. He is preparing us for communion – for joy, for nearness, for life shared without distance or division.

Many of us have been taught to imagine eternity in abstract or distant terms. Yet Jesus repeatedly spoke of the kingdom in the language of tables and banquets, of rooms filled with guests, of abundance meant to be received. These images invite us to see that the future God is bringing about is not less personal, but more – not less embodied, but more fully alive.

As we come to this week, we do not rush ahead to the end of the story. Instead, we allow the promise of the feast to quietly shape how we live and hope even now.

For when love is nearing its fulfillment, something begins to soften within us. Gratitude grows more easily. Generosity widens. Joy, sometimes quietly and sometimes unexpectedly, begins to take up more space in the soul.

This is not the joy of denial or forced optimism. It is the steady joy that grows wherever the presence of Christ is welcomed and trusted.

The wedding feast is both promise and invitation.

Even now, God is preparing His people – through longing, through love, through the quiet ways His life is already at work within us. The future union toward which Scripture points is not disconnected from the present; it is the flowering of the same love that has been drawing us all along.

We enter this time slowly and with openness, as those stepping into a great hall where the table has already been set.

There is nothing to prove. Nothing to force. Only an invitation to notice and to receive.

Blessed are those who are invited to the wedding supper of the Lamb.

May this week awaken holy joy, deepen your hope, and steady your heart in the love that is even now preparing the feast.

Group Reflection

Read aloud

In a moment, I will read a few discussion prompts. Each person will have a moment to share anything they would like to reflect. We will go around the room to provide each person with space, but nobody should feel like there is any pressure. If you have nothing to say, simply pass. As we share together:

- We keep our responses brief.
- We do not try to fix or correct one another.
- We allow moments of silence between speakers.
- We trust that simple honesty is enough.

Leader gently guides the group using the prompts below.

1. **Prompt 1**

   When you hear the image of *the wedding feast of the Lamb,* what sense of hope or longing rises within you?

   Allow brief, unhurried sharing.

2. **Prompt 2**

   Where have you noticed small signs of joy or renewal beginning to grow in your life during this season?

   Allow sharing. Do not rush to fill silence.

3. **Optional Prompt 3**

   What would it look like for you to live this week as someone who is already invited to the table?

   Use only if the conversation feels natural and unforced.

Transition to Stillness

Read aloud

As our voices settle, we begin to turn our attention more fully toward God's presence among us.

Let us become still together.

Settling into Stillness

Read aloud

As our voices quiet, we allow the room to grow still.

There is nothing we need to accomplish in this moment.
Nothing we need to prove.
Nothing we need to force.

We simply become present together.

Let us become still.

Pause here for 60–90 seconds of shared silence.

Allow the silence to feel unhurried. If the room feels slightly restless at first, do not rush forward. The settling is part of the work.

Opening Prayer

Read aloud

Faithful Bridegroom,

You who have called us and kept us, draw us again into Your presence. As we gather, quiet what still feels hurried within us and awaken in us a deeper readiness for Your joy.

Thank You for the patient love that has carried us to this moment – for the ways You have been forming us, steadying us, and drawing us nearer to Your heart.

Where our hope has felt distant, bring it close. Where our joy has felt small or uncertain, gently enlarge it by Your Spirit.

Teach us to live as those who are already invited – watchful, grateful, and at rest in Your faithful love.

We belong to You, and we welcome the life You are preparing for Your people.

Amen.

Becoming Aware of the Breath

Read aloud

We remain seated in stillness.

Feet grounded.
Hands resting gently.

If it feels comfortable, we allow our eyes to close.

We begin by simply noticing the breath.

Air entering.
Air leaving.

After a few natural breaths, we allow the rhythm to slow slightly.

We inhale gently through the nose.
We exhale slowly through the nose.

If it feels natural, let the exhale be just a little longer than the inhale.

There is no need to force the breath.
We are not trying to breathe perfectly.

We are simply allowing the body to settle into a quieter rhythm.

Inhale… slowly.
Exhale… gently.

Unhurried.
Steady.
Present.

Remain here for about 2–3 minutes.

If the mind begins to wander, simply return our attention to the quiet rhythm of the breath.

In this gentle awareness, we allow the body to soften . . . and the heart to become attentive.

Breathing the Prayer

Read aloud

Continue breathing slowly and gently.

Keeping the same quiet rhythm we have already found, begin to let a simple prayer accompany the rhythm.

As we inhale slowly through the nose, we pray silently:

You are here.

As we exhale gently:

We are Yours.

Inhale…

You are here.

Exhale…

We are Yours.

We do not rush the words.

If the breath and the words do not match perfectly, we let the words soften and follow the natural rhythm of the breath.

We remain unhurried.

Continue for several breaths.

The Breath of Belonging

Now we allow the deeper promise to rest on the breath.

As we inhale:

We are our Beloved's…

As we exhale:

…and our Beloved is ours.

Slowly.

Gently.

Steady and unforced.

Again.

Inhale…

We are our Beloved's…

Exhale…

…and our Beloved is ours.

If the mind wanders, we simply return.

If the words fade for a moment, we begin again.

We are not trying to create closeness.

We are resting in what has already been spoken over us.

Remain here for several breaths.

The Breath of Quiet

Now, release the words.

We continue breathing slowly and gently.

Christ stands among His people – steady, attentive, near.

We rest together in the quiet.

Remain in silence for about 60–90 seconds.

Re-Gathering

Together, softly, we say once:

We are our Beloved's, and our Beloved is ours.

We let the words settle.

And we remain still.

Hearing the Word

Read aloud

We remain seated in stillness.

Our breathing stays slow and gentle.

We do not hurry this moment.

As the Scripture is read, we listen together.

We are not listening to analyze. We are not listening to master the text.

We are simply receiving the words as they are spoken among us.

If a word or phrase draws our attention, we notice it gently and let it remain.

Stay relaxed.
Stay unhurried.
Stay present.

Scripture Readings

- **Revelation 16: 6 – 9**

  Leader reads slowly and clearly.

  Then I heard what sounded like a great multitude, like the roar of rushing waters and like loud peals of thunder, shouting:
  "Hallelujah!
  For our Lord God Almighty reigns.
  Let us rejoice and be glad

and give him glory!
For the wedding of the Lamb has come,
and his bride has made herself ready.
Fine linen, bright and clean,
was given her to wear."
Then the angel said to me, "Write this: Blessed are those who are invited to the wedding supper of the Lamb!" And he added, "These are the true words of God."

Pause in silence — about 20–30 seconds.

Leader reads again, slightly more slowly.

Longer silence — about 30–45 seconds.

Leader reads a third time, unhurried and steady.

Remain in silence — about 60 seconds.

Repeat the same exercise with any of these additional scriptures:

- **Revelation 21: 2 – 4**
  I saw the Holy City, the new Jerusalem, coming down out of heaven from God, prepared as a bride beautifully dressed for her husband. And I heard a loud voice from the throne saying, "Look! God's dwelling place is now among the people, and he

will dwell with them. They will be his people, and God himself will be with them and be their God. 'He will wipe every tear from their eyes. There will be no more death'[] or mourning or crying or pain, for the old order of things has passed away."

- **Isaiah 25: 6 – 8**

  On this mountain the Lord Almighty will prepare
  a feast of rich food for all peoples,
  a banquet of aged wine—
  the best of meats and the finest of wines.
  On this mountain he will destroy
  the shroud that enfolds all peoples,
  the sheet that covers all nations;
  he will swallow up death forever.
  The Sovereign Lord will wipe away the tears
  from all faces;
  he will remove his people's disgrace
  from all the earth.
  The Lord has spoken.

Interior Noticing

Read aloud

We remain in the quiet for a moment longer.

There is nothing we need to figure out.

We simply notice what has gently risen within us as we listened.

We stay relaxed.
We stay unhurried.
We remain attentive.

Gentle Reflection

Without forcing words, notice:

What word or phrase quietly drew our attention?

Pause. Allow silence first before any sharing.

If it feels natural, we may briefly speak the word or phrase that stood out to us.

We keep our sharing simple and unhurried.

After a few responses or a short pause, continue.

Where did we sense warmth . . . or perhaps a place of resistance?

Pause again. Allow brief sharing if appropriate.

We do not need to explain why.

We simply notice.

After another pause.

What, if anything, felt like invitation?

Allow silence to carry this moment.

Holding the Moment

We resist the urge to analyze or resolve.

God often speaks most clearly in what quietly lingers.

We allow what has surfaced to remain gently before Him.

Short silence — about 30–45 seconds.

Receiving the Promise

Together, softly, we say:

We are our Beloved's, and our Beloved is ours.

Repeat once more, slowly.

We are our Beloved's, and our Beloved is ours.

We let the words settle among us.

Brief silence.

Closing Prayer

Read aloud

Faithful Bridegroom,

You have been with us in every step of this journey. From the first awakening of desire to this quiet vision of the feast, Your love has remained steady and near.

Thank You for the ways You have been forming us – drawing us, simplifying us, teaching us to abide in Your presence.

Keep our hearts watchful and at peace as we continue to live in the space between promise and fulfillment. Where joy has begun to take root in us, let it grow. Where hope still feels small or fragile, strengthen it by Your faithful Spirit.

Make us a people who live as those already invited – grateful, steady, and ready to welcome Your life each day.

We belong to You, and we rest in the love that is preparing all things for joy.

Amen.

Resting in the Quiet

We remain together in stillness for one final moment.

When the time feels right, the leader may softly say:

We return gently to one another.

Participants may slowly open their eyes.

Take a moment to notice the room again.

Notice one another.

When ready, simple conversation may resume naturally.

There is no need to rush away.

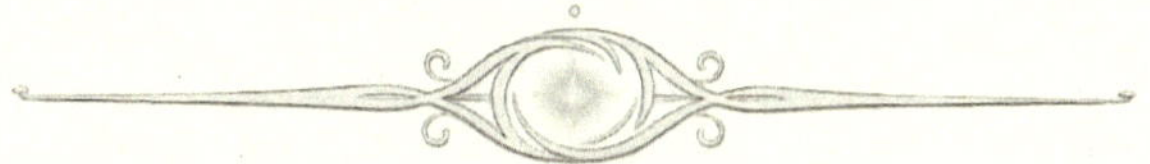

Returning to the Heart of the Bridegroom

This five-week journey through the imagery of the Bride of Christ has invited you to sit with that truth—not as a metaphor, but as the deepest reality beneath all others. Scripture presents the Christian life not simply as disciples following a teacher, but as a Bride preparing for union with her Bridegroom. Every page of the biblical story bends toward this moment of communion.

You have explored this longing through five movements. Together, these movements sketch the shape of the spiritual life: awakening, surrender, purification, belonging, and joy.

But they do not end here.

The Bride is not simply waiting for a future day – she is being formed, moment by moment, into love. Your journey continues each time you pause to listen, each time you surrender a small fear, each time you choose trust over self-reliance, each time you receive God's delight as truth rather than wishful thinking.

A Final Blessing

May the One who calls you "Beloved" make His home in your heart. May your life be shaped by His gentleness, your desires purified by His love, your hope anchored in His promise.

May the Bridegroom awaken in you a joy that no darkness can diminish and a longing that leads you ever more deeply into union with Him.

And may you come to know, beyond words and beyond striving, this most beautiful truth:

You belong to Him.

And He delights that you do.

Amen.

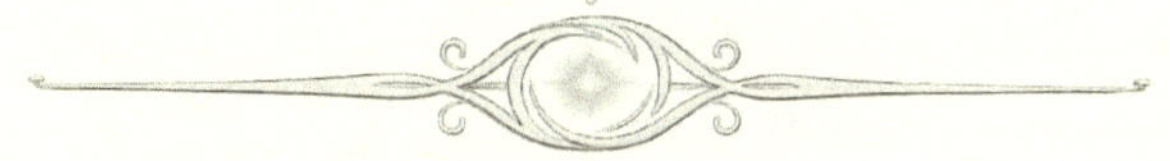

The Principles Behind the Practices

The Christian Contemplative Tradition

The practices in this guide (silence, attentive breathing, and slow, prayerful reading of Scripture) may feel unfamiliar to some readers. Yet none of these practices are new. Each has deep roots in the historic life of the Church.

From the earliest centuries, followers of Christ have recognized that spiritual formation involves not only what we believe, but how we learn to attend to God with our whole selves. The Christian contemplative tradition developed as one way the Church has sought to live faithfully into the invitation of Scripture:

"Be still, and know that I am God." (Psalm 46:10)

This guide stands within that stream.

What follows is a brief description of the theological and historical foundations beneath the practices used throughout this study.

Silence: Making Room to Attend

Throughout Scripture, silence is repeatedly associated with reverence, attentiveness, and trust in God's presence.

The psalmist writes:

"For God alone my soul waits in silence." (Psalm 62:1)

Jesus Himself regularly withdrew to quiet places to pray (Luke 5:16). The early desert Christians of the third and fourth centuries continued this pattern, understanding that silence was not empty space but a way of becoming more attentive to God.

In this guide, silence is not treated as a technique for achieving altered states or emotional effects. It is simply the intentional laying down of noise—external and internal—so that the heart can listen more fully. Silence creates space in which the Word of God may be received rather than merely analyzed.

Breath and the Prayerful Body

Breath awareness has long been part of Christian prayer. The biblical languages themselves connect breath and spirit: the Hebrew *ruach* and the Greek *pneuma* both carry the dual meaning of breath, wind, and spirit.

Early Christian writers often noted the natural connection between steady breathing and a settled interior life. In the Eastern Christian tradition, forms of the Jesus Prayer were sometimes gently coordinated with the rhythm of breathing—not as a mechanical exercise, but as a way of helping the whole person participate in prayer.

In this guide, breathing practices are intentionally simple and unforced. They are not presented as techniques for control or self-optimization. Rather, they serve one humble purpose: to help the body grow still enough for the heart to become attentive.

The aim is not to manipulate experience, but to support the natural quieting that allows prayerful awareness to deepen.

Lectio Divina: Listening to Scripture Slowly

The slow, prayerful reading of Scripture—often called *Lectio Divina* ("sacred reading")—has been practiced in the Church for well over a millennium. Monastic communities in particular developed this approach as a way of engaging Scripture not only for information, but for transformation.

Traditionally, Lectio involves:

- reading the text slowly
- listening for a word or phrase that draws attention
- resting with the text in prayer
- and allowing the Word to shape the heart

This guide follows that same spirit. The repeated readings of Scripture are not meant to produce new interpretations or novel insights. Instead, they create space for participants to receive the text personally and prayerfully.

In this way, Scripture moves from being something we study to something that begins to dwell within us.

Interior Noticing: The Work of Attention

Christian spiritual writers have long emphasized the importance of watchfulness over the movements of the heart. The desert fathers spoke of *nepsis* – a gentle, prayerful awareness of what rises within us in God's presence.

This is not introspection for its own sake, nor is it an invitation to self-criticism. Rather, it is a posture of honest attentiveness before God.

In this guide, "interior noticing" simply invites participants to observe what they become aware of during prayer:

- a word that lingers
- a sense of peace or resistance
- a memory or longing that surfaces

These moments are not forced or analyzed. They are simply noticed and gently offered to God.

A Final Reassurance

All of these practices share a common aim: to help believers love God with heart, soul, mind, and strength (Mark 12:30). They do not replace Scripture, the gathered church, or the ordinary means of grace. Rather, they serve as quiet supports that help many people become more attentive to the presence and work of Christ.

Nothing in this guide depends on special techniques or spiritual achievement. Growth in the Christian life remains, as it has always been, the work of God's grace within us.

Our role is simply to make ourselves available.

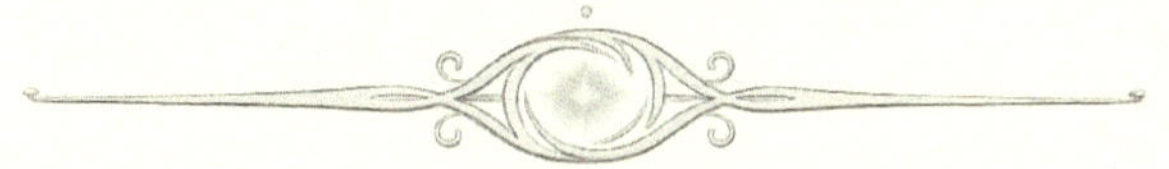

Thank You for Walking This Journey

You have completed The Bride of Christ Contemplation — a journey of awakening, longing, and hope. This guide was crafted for those who seek not only to learn about God, but to encounter Him. If something within you has stirred, softened, or awakened during these weeks, give thanks: the Spirit is already shaping you into the image of Christ.

Continue Growing with Symbol & Silence

Symbol & Silence exists to help Christians explore the depths of Scripture with clarity, humility, and contemplative joy. Each week, new essays and reflections are published on Substack — always free, always accessible.

To learn more or to join, visit: http://www.symbolandsilence.com where you will find Bible studies, devotionals, pastoral resources, ministry guides, artwork, and teaching tools.

www.ingramcontent.com/pod-product-compliance
Lightning Source LLC
LaVergne TN
LVHW051009080826
845145LV00009B/2538
* 9 7 8 1 9 7 2 0 8 8 0 1 2 *